blood

snow

WAVE BOOKS   SEATTLE & NEW YORK

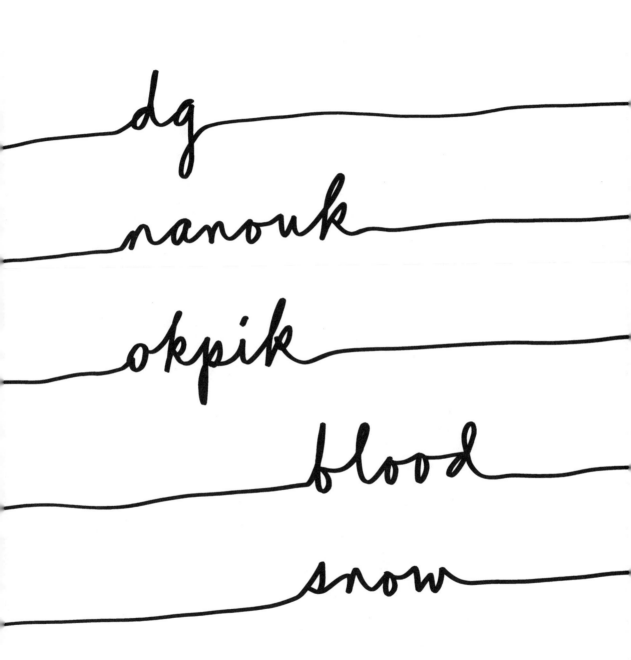

dg

nanouk

okpik

blood

snow

Published by Wave Books

www.wavepoetry.com

Copyright © 2022 by dg nanouk okpik

Wave Books titles are distributed to the trade by

Consortium Book Sales and Distribution

Phone: 800-283-3572 | SAN 631-760X

Library of Congress Cataloging-in-Publication Data

Names: Okpik, Dg Nanouk, author.

Title: Blood snow / dg nanouk okpik.

Description: First edition. | Seattle : Wave Books, [2022]

Identifiers: LCCN 2022020002 | ISBN 9781950268641 (hardcover)

ISBN 9781950268634 (paperback)

Subjects: LCGFT: Poetry.

Classification: LCC PS3615.K75 B57 2022 | DDC 811/.6—dc23/eng/20220422

LC record available at https://lccn.loc.gov/2022020002

Designed by Crisis

Printed in the United States of America

9 8 7 6 5 4 3 2 1

First Edition

Wave Books 102

blood

snow

Foregrass

A toil of one inside me:
She/I cast a thick,
                         sod-wall
time out of mind,
out of sync, off course.

I see: Forgrass little blue,
little stemmed flowers,
                         light mottled
purple yellow centered star,
She/I go there to the egg-cortex: Nest.

Change into her/my parka hood

She/I wear a time meter: earth's surface
Let it be into the outer cornice,
                    to measure the nebulous.

A timing belt, bearing teeth, gage
turning
rusty sprockets, diamond-dust covered
She/I measure to pinpoint a sounding line underneath,

the sea depth of my/her childhood. Restricted to no particular,
time, only emerald-green ocean, sea or lake.

I see: poisonous buttercups,
    soda ash from ceramics,
    glass black smooth;
    I stand to keep time.

Choosing Inflorescence

Her heedless gaze dilates,
pinpointing her name *kiktugiak*, mosquito.
Her sucking grip on hindered flowers.

Three hundred sixteen whirs
per second twitch, twinge, and circulate;
turquoise wings rotating and cupping air.

Male and female *kiktugiak* slide in—
dance synchronizing their wings in air.
A dance w/ her sights
on mortal daze or night flashes.

No, it was not her design
for she did not know of such things,
as gruesome, or as natural in grisly terms.

But maybe, in flickered movement,
she made it through the blister-rust season,
because of a methane metallic mirror of spirits in flight.

It took all the blood in her belly
to fly around the sick white pine, with blister
swelling on twigs and bark of rust season.

Her itch-poked legs gingerly stepping
on roots and pinecones, it seemed like a flashpoint,
she felt sick alighting on the yellow ash.

But it was her choosing inflorescence,
of the spiked crown lopseed, her shaking abdomen,
and instinct for white nectar, she knew once before
above a rainstorm puddle breeding, then laying eggs.

Anthropocene Years

Here Cape Lisburne
Or maybe not there.

Kaktovik then
on New Siberian Islands.

Here not here.
Elsewhere but not anywhere.

But somewhere like Cape Chelyuskin;
or White Island; yes, set the route due north.

As my compass taps out of bearing in circles.
Here Novaya Zemlya. A gyroscope.

Here on the boreal island, Norway.
Wherever it is it's warm.

Here choking on acidic air.

Here Greenland, Jan Mayen.
No it's Disko.

Here Canada.
Baffin Island.

Grinnell Lake.
Minto Inlet.

Place fogged lenses on telescopic eyes.
Here brilliant colors of pollution so high.

Here in the melt sun, heaving waters of ocean and sea.
Here start ending double-rate heat   to sweat & yet, not yet.

Here wake up there not here.

Early Morning Sky Blue Pink

AT KNIK ARM w/ SILT CLAY QUICKSAND

On Knik Arm, there with a dark moon on the rise—
I stood awestruck, once, as the sun floated into the east.

Sky blue pink sky blue pink sky blue snow,
fell in perfect repose, I sit cross-legged lotus style.

The morning dream in a distance, an inukshuk,
young-old-women of igneous rock standing

at rest, tall and safe. In the sunglow I roll
a handful of ice silt clay, roll it in my hands until

they're red-rose red—I don't let them bleed.
Let them feel with the texture of each grain.

I'm a round ball; minute ball.
A blossom ball of future-past-present.

My eyes flow, eyes of tears to the angels & archangels,
as I make wet, dry, warm, cold & fire flame. I'm off kilter.

I am twixt & torn with emotive thoughts of mortality.
Will this be the time?

Instead of going there, my mindfulness changes.
Rubbing 6 cents together life is richer in spans.

So, I'm riding the storm which engulfs me
all of a sudden: I bundle beat an Inuit drum;

with a snare string, red dots circling the polar star.
I see in my head daily this drum and this song:

Sky blue pink sky blue pink sky pink blues. I realize the silt
is not clay, but quicksand, in which I'm neck high.

Enforced Measures

Along with 1,731 cots lined in rows
lies a man named Ebulu.
He's quarantined in a tent of canvas walls.
Something catches him—
Hyena yapping—pitches rising,
with laughter, like he did on rice wine.
But tonight, it's the contortions
of hamstring cramps that burn.
He watches for 40 days of detention
of Jackals and Ebola.
At once, he flees and hitches a ride
on a packed Rover,
Like a black snake. He's gaunt,
gray-fleshed and skinny.
Once an ebony headed to anywhere.
He dreams of a place of small children,
keep at bay the conquerers. It happens:
as he floats above, he's a man and fierce.
Now, ostracized leaving the imposed isolation
running in tall grass, grinning;
the boys chasing the girls with a garden snake.
Runs for the airport and departs in the cargo
bed of a jet airliner. The slat wood fence

around the makeshift infirmary,
twinges and jolts of cold sweat trembles;
came to be quick. He knew it well.
He wants only care and the freedom
of trotting with the wild dogs hunting,
an empty cart hooked to the back.

Horizon at Duck Camp

The dog mine ghosts yapping my name

I did not cry. I just stared,

like a stone

on a river's bottom

watching the ice melt

on the surface. Spring thaw on the Colville.

I stared until my knuckles were purple

my tongue swollen

my ears deafened by howls

screaming Iisagrik coming for me,

Peter Paul, Johnny Billy, Edna.

Like a frozen sheefish the feeling of cold,

aluminum foil to a filled molar

it twinges metallic.

Pulsing my toes the inua spirit,

you asked me what does it feel like @ 60 below?

I did not answer.

I don't know.

An elusive seal shark patrolling the freshwater sea.

Like a polar ice bear grinding his teeth

into a seal's skull. First an old

genetic memory burnishes

in the smell, blood of snow.

In the ice fields,

a nightmare of travel

beating me raw in red cloud-storms.

Mashed to the cheeks,

tongues & lisping lips.

Razor-stubbed eyes water out of the nose,

I blood-a-beat

the night a tar-lathered road,

into the first-grow of dog.

A mist of black & blue fog,

evaporating the plastic shield

the mind stalls & stalks

the inuk as the snow machine blades cut

an elder caribou trail

freshly from the inside arm,

at the ice-forge end,

the horizon line of sea & land,

where the sky meets the turf,

blends any field sight I hunt.

A wolverine haunts me,

his nails curled taut like a rusted root.

Wire wrapped around his neck.

One learned of suicide by finding

a bloated head tied to a limb

of an alder tree.

By flinching a glimpse

of a 17-year-old man quartered left to rot

with eyes red   red.

Petrified Melt

I candle
the liquid
myriad maze,
pain rising
water levels.
In salt.
I measure my
temperature
in windchill factor.
Dust born from
old glacial ice
snow melting I
with cupped hands
to mouth &
cupped to lips
drink the salt sea.

Dissolving
ocean,
I pray for more land,
to mend my melee
fused together by
an *abatement in weather*.
Tell me again what to say:

Adoption

Copper

Coal

Oil

Oil oil

Natural gas

I collect

The ability

To heal the

De   struc   tion

~~Extract~~

~~Extract~~

~~Extract~~

a whistling buoy

a float alone

in spring thaw

A Glacial Oil World

A gray-black storm lies low, above the sea.
A 78 mile per hour windchill shatters any
water into icebergs, as I drown in my own element.
Rustling waves rolling me back to this massive
breakup outside and in. It glides past me blue-green,
blue-turquoise, collisions of pinnacles and pressure
points, which pinch. Volcano ash, radiation and
chemo ruin the physical. Old frozen cliffs, hoarfrost
lungs, clefts of monastic bergs adrift. I cough, cough
up bowels of human limits of sanity, sounds of gale
winds rifting the clapboard house I call home, as my
lungs carry my brain; carry my heart, and innards,
hands and feet; I hand palm the distance of sky and light.

> Cut Yukon salmon
> In my eyes, the river flows
> The scent of burnt birch

Necklaced Whalebone

As I toss & roll
these bones
at the 2nd & 3rd vertebrae
the cracked curvity of my neck
where something
of a   wing   fused.
Bowed   & fossilized
merging kink-bended
wrongly. Then merged
bended & slouched
in a hunchbacked crooked
pain.   Into a pinged
pang   where needles
& cracks at my side
the forced   hanging. Sluiced
movement of ivory
scalloped cervixes at the
nape it snaps, snaps.
I rebound   at the fear
& instinctively   quake
with vanquished surrender.
In numbness I wake then
mumble you're part of me

now   leave. It slaps its tail
then   a V formation follows
but decelerates   the sea waves
source   of   vigor 11,500 years old.

A Year Dot

FOR ARTHUR SZE

(*Qin*) *Dim Sum* equivalent to *dot, speck, heart*

Stone piled on stone I finish my meal.
In this early sunrise I see a shadow where a cairn of rocks
stood in the eastern light.

In late morning, I lit red candles and placed them
next to a three-hinged mirror, as a way of seeing
shadows of shadows.

Milkweed grows on the side of the road in ditches,
reminiscent of professor's soft words, amazing the brilliant
contemplation and thought pattern as you learn, slowly.

In my body neuron-zipped words and more words.
My lexicon building from nothing to something good.
Embossed tattoos like small notes on sheet music.

Dots and lines, strands and strings I rest on the note D
increased by one half as my orchestra director signals,
dashes and spaces for letters as grace notes in Morse code.

Notes in staccato igniting instrumental waves of burning wood,
a fiery spark over and speck dust played in harmonics,
as a coot hovers over a brook dives in comes back with a fish.

No one would ever know its true beauty and calmness
the setting sun across an arctic lake unless it is witnessed.
As speckled day owls, brants and mergansers float in the sunset.

To learn you must be open, diligent, and willing to be an individual.
11,000 murres with webbed feet land also without any fear of predators.
But still, on the page grow spotted mushrooms and morels.

Examine the distortion and effects of the warming earth.
The change of the ice age with purpose as the warming earth today
But I take heart in sun along with the core of a ginkgo tree's light.

Shaman Boy: Utqiagvik, Circa 1878

1

When the snapping of hip creates a boy,
by extracting splinters & keeping the sinew,
from dead-over-bones, he lived as an old one.

Angakoq boy waits on the jagged cusp of a blue walrus,
on the point of moratorium, a point of shudder,
where no one is designated a slender pick.

A spider mite blends into the fall cranberry leaves,
the first growth of a tooth breaks through the gum
of a marmot:

his ila: my relative by blood;
> *by marriage, or name;*
> *his companion & friend;*
> *soon to have a partner;*
> *his part of a whole; in a whale fluke*
> *which will become his co-participant.*
> *In this world, in future time & space.*
> *This becomes his place namesake, this place.*
> *A name of old, 100 years erased, then whole again.*
> > *Utqiagvik.*

2

Angakoq boy abolished the storehouse of bear tongues,
then tied them in a knot wrapped in ptarmigan feathers for
his father as an effigy to wear on his duck-skin belt.
It flails & flutters sometimes eating roots using his webbed feet to swim.

A stigmata of birthmarks, a freckled boy,
So small his flat-bones, cartilage sinew strength,
he stands in the center at the front of the line of birds,
he connects his spliced ribs like bone toggles, the boy leader.

> *Angakoq sees the boy's eyes and then he*
> *throws, he turns, his wrist sideways to lash whip;*
> *in the air practicing for sledge dogs with a high spirit.*

Ice balls relieved the boy's stricken ache when he got TB.
As strong as he was healed by his medicine mind in
a dream sweat.

Late last fall the year he recalled splitting ninepins of pinewood.
As sap shellacked the contour of mammoth Skin Armor as his baby
fat left; 8 years later he turned into the chieftain who lived
in a new white *tupiq/tent with a chosen wolf/wife named Kivalina.*
As a man he became from wolves was named Shishmaref of Utqiagvik.

Fate Map

If I'm a left-eyed flounder
I live in the icy-green depths.
Not ever having to worry about the lee tide
going where wind bellows across inlet.
I swim in circles and speak Inupiaq
in circumlocution as the shamans sing in
tongues. Olden people lived in the cliffs
dissolving now into scribed fate-maps.

Chunky furrowed calves' goggles help me see—
right-eyed in confidence.

Light Years of Humans

*

absence/presence
may be a way

humans in deep verse

a mockingbird
tangled inside
a body

*

Spring Thaw

A remnant conceals
things I can't
change, a blue
glacial memory
reveals:
        light's sharp edges—
                I lean.
As if my body—
subdued
by brittle, gutter, brim
ice. Finding a chickadee's
feather on a snowflake,
while lost in slumberous,
smooth, blue, smoke.

        I awaken to a chirping,
        flock fly overhead.
        Indeed grace.

Hollow Hands

You dig with hollow hands,
with hammer & tongs
carve out my wrists:
metacarpals, fingers & thumb.

At times my song muffles—as if
snapping your knuckles were deep.
The talons of the falcon is a hand.
The bird takes flight with messages
carried: Under Erasure. Nihilism.

Whiteout Polar Bears

Dead on—in the night sky,
or stuck in the deep web,
bear stars exist. Name the
bone piles on the marsh
heaving like the Chukchi
sea-pure-ice-white and
Arctic air rising. Fifty miles
of open water floating.
I'm a carcass with
marrow bones 5x's an ice
bear at 1,500 lb. and 9 feet
tall. One swipe of my paw
you're neck-snapped, to the ice,
melt ground, cheek to red
ice stream. I glance across
the whiteness to myself.

Ice Age Two

Eskimo women
who sat on driftwood logs . . .
what they most dread.
—BARRY LOPEZ

Sunken sod of whalebone,
earth houses rising,
out of feathered sea
         water.

Children's children,
aunties as mothers
rapidly fading,
hauntingly, drooped faces
         dangling.

Quickly now!
    See it now—
    As petals of wild
    roses and dewdrops—

Root rot
from
nothing but lakes
of methane gas

Polar Bear Lost

The Little People brought south
winds with pollution. As the polar
thunder starts in a rip-crackle-
roaring, across, on January 1st
2018 in Santa Fe just as
Ursus Maritimus. Mixing
and mingling with man. No Fear.
Dead on with blank stares and thin
boned with thick matted hair.

> Beer and soda cans
> Thunderbirds take flight northwards
> Mud tan polar cubs

Man and the Little People

The Little People interacting
with man brought the east wind
dominating foul, uncertain
patterns of methane, through
seas of driftwood timbers, for
ribs of earth mounds slide
sea cliffs, whales quaver in
vexation of puzzle, through
koan dynamics, hex meddling
of heat/thaw.

> mud and gravel no
> landmass only mercury
> earth's axis teeters

Fossil Fuel Embers

At Red Dog Mine boys and girls
(displaced) as trade dogs
for the Yankee sailors, slaves,
as large gul-guled wooden ships—
started by taking coal. Red
from dog mine. Black lungs
shiny in dead crawls. Each death,
I cut a notch on the driftwood
log, in my home, where I burn
because it makes embers.

> way in and one way out
> blackwood cooked slow over done
> skies whale gray-blue

Frightening Acid Flakes

If stars could bend
white-blue, copper, brass,
in sterling
moonshine
I could see caribou prancing onto moss floors;
wouldn't be at all encompassing.
Snowflakes fall and land in the cold
face of a monster, a split flame-tongued
beast, from the frigid, notched depths,
living on village ledge keeps the people in
unsafe. They find peace in the fire,
lava-orange-red to the face of a Kaktovik
umialik.

Feathers, fins and fur
Frozen tundra bare night sky
Here gone lies double deep

Her/My Things

Her things—
      whalebone;

      antler;

      ivory;

      stone;

      hide;

      wood.

My things—
      pencil;

      wax crayon;

Her things—
      crude ( ) words;

      sinew.

      Shit. Shit. Shit.

      The bowels

      of self belonging

      to creation is

      scintillating, yet—

      of mortal grossness.

Twilight Pain

I have died so many midnight moons,
most of night soil not realized until later.
In peculiar sleep, caught by a night-latched
mind like some dark dew on the breaching hips,
resemble a red blossom, birth & blood is the rose.
I pang & I hurt but a summons in black snow,
of ukpik, calls as white snow owls on black earth melt,
our catching eyes lock in deadbolt time & ukpik calls
moonlight across tundra, on a level plain
with a photoreceptor stimulated by light
floating to the blue hue of dawn.
At daybreak, my night person fades,
my drowsiness & lethargic body
rises to alleviate the deep
nightlong pain of restlessness.
It's the light through purple celestial bodies
belonging to the daytime,
diurnal cycle, of wavelengths dancing
in & out nightmarish, lunacy.
Dancing with my namesake, there.
Living in the sienna's myriad
mazes lost beyond found, alive but mostly dead.
I am brushstrokes of a painting half-finished.

What is not clear to me is the order
by which humans now go by.
Sometimes my tunicate, saclike body
fills with ill plague.
Illness disperses, dispels, vanishes in paint on a canvas
no different than multicolored wildflowers.
Distinguished only to a few,
not all flowers accounted for or named just yet.
There for a reason. I don't know why,
how, when they came,
when they chose to leave
but I do know & wait.
I live in a dugout in the cliffs next to the ocean,
bluffs receding filling with seawater rising
from melting glacial ice. Across the inlet seal island
not far from my dugout.
They bark and sun themselves all day,
but are in constant fear of losing ground to walrus.
The tons of blubber could squash a seal
out of sheer creature comfort.
Walrus take over any small island
rolling around in the sand;
waiting for the coming schools of fish
voraciously hungry, grunting to the sway of wind,
sea of the long twilight hours.

In a Lock of Hair

In a lock of hair becoming a spine-like tendon,
in stagnant blood *might I find*—I don't know.
Liquid, light, glass grooved and lashed together:

a brown feathered and horned-angel owl,
damned in a part of breast-cusped armpit.

Where spindle, shanks, polished by gray silt, dash
ruined my middle chest, caves in. When a wasp
nest unravels the gray paper like a head of lettuce.

A corroded filament of a white bear's heart
shines in warm snow like frozen fireflies stuck
in the air still yellow. A bulldozer digs the taiga.

A Nuwuk whale captain hones the shoreline,
wishes the whale-people to come: scouts first,
middle males, females and young then older whales.

Shades and drifts of tangled oceans, labyrinths in
navigational mapping turn upon itself like dragon's tail.
Right ventricle then left ventricle boils like copper in vats.

Radiation of a lumbar sack and coccyx, wires drip dip
coils, inverted cones, dug for sifts & wood black peat soil &
as five red robins' beaks funnel earthworms in haste.

Confluence

Continuous flowing pouring rain
drenches my body: cold yet nice,
nice enough to create blossom and rot.

Purple iris and fireweed out my open window;
a throng of Knik River raging. Sparkles of light
into Cook Inlet. A sprinkle of ocean spray on my face.

I am human: an ego-syntonic woman;
water; I am contradiction, water & blood
on a page of words joining; meeting; in union;
a collision of squid ink; salmon & paper.

Crow's Caw Echo Echo

I

In the hills and juniper berries.   Crow's sleeping.

In his dream,   he found or stole   from   Cormorant

          now ridiculed by Marmot.   At Cormorant's nest

                    I evaporate in a minute,   in an unsettling minute.

A crashed dream of a strange

Crow,   a conjuring   crow-person,

or something-like-a-crow,   I don't remember or don't

          forget.

Crow landed   on a tarred   chipped road,

talking to Cormorant about why he ate so much.

5 bushels of hooligan   early in the day at the Kodiak island.

Cormorant boasting   didn't notice

Crow stealing   his berries   in his high nest.

After Cormorant noticed   his bounty was gone.

He started shouting   to all who'd

listen on an aluminum   totem pole.

There sat a razorbill and puffin   (they didn't believe Crow).

Nobody ever believed Crow

"You're so foolish and gullible

always hanging   out with Crow!"   "CROW!" said Marmot

That night,   a human was camping

in the Brooks Range.

left his fire going.

The fire jumps from wind

as

boiling a storm,   the fire lit flicks,

all the underbrush

dried from recent   warming earth.

II

The fire   burned fierce, quickly & cornered Marmot,

Marmot   taunted   Crow.

Mocked Crow & Crow's   voracious   appetite

for   food   with   wild tails

as they flew away.   They left Crow behind   on the shiny

cold pole,   Crow with his   head down   pecking.

On his bluish-purple   black feathers with stomach

bloated;   he concocted a   tall explanation.

I'll tell those people   they know   nothing.

Crow flew to the land   of wooden pallets,

& wrecked Japanese barges.   Drifting   scattered

into deep forges   forges like mountains of skyscrapers;

Crow listened to nasal   murmuring ghosts.

They spooked   him back into flight,   Crow sees a man

chainsawing boards; counting in a tongue   he   heard

before,   flying across the sky   of vapor red trails.   Crow

tracing a steel-pretty bird   with metallic wings,

scathing blood-blue   sky surely, nobody

would listen.

It Cuts

Their sliced feet drag across razor-burnt snow,
their soles laying bloody tracks marking a course laid out
for yellow ice-worms, mosquito larvae, and Steller's eider.

I am conjuring violet-fire the head and foot of a ptarmigan,
tied to a string to which I interlace my *kamiks*, darn tundra grass,
where gray wanders the land. In solidification of a raindrop.

NIL Ink & Paper

The architecture of a Russian sage bush,
A hornet hovering & landing: the one
of many: a concourse sound in minuets
of verbal opus, indulging space & time triangle.

I examine boundless expanse of nature.
I am nomadic in my mind-sense. I am someone.
I am nothing-but, some nihil, white—paper—ink.

Mind Warp

I

A black-browed albatross flung into a storm forced of solar wind.

A bird strapped by the chin so tight his maker white knuckled, as if he performed a lobotomy on the seabird. A surgery takes all memory away of fish, water, ice, and land. A grand seabird broken from the lost traces of old stories to mark in vigor a whole flock.

No human responds only with Rorschach tests.

II

Stories long as intestines can release buttercups if teased.

Tubular, long, guts murmur with waste as the shorelines reveal trash, oil-dead birds, broken beer-bottle glass, and an empty bucket.

No ducks this year. "Accept it," the bird said in my ear. I know it comes and goes at times as warp wind blows. A flock of black scared birds takes flight, from fright, does not fight it. Rather encompasses it. The black-black birds circle and settle on the cliffs of the Pacific Ocean of the Gulf of Alaska.

I saw: One lone old Albatross landing on a twisted cable of an electrical line.

III

Say: I am going mad;
Scratch head tiptoed ankle crack;
Say: Crisscross double dutch;
A shell shaker in my sleep warped dreams
Say: Chronotherapy in a rainbow,
Say: Chrysalis pupa.

Expedition Mars

The landscape of the brain closes its eyes
to see the brightest red of Mars
reflecting millions of miles away.
Some human eyes, noses, mouths & touch is lost.
Infused infliction of what a whole mind body,
sheer willpower can do of who we are;
it develops if need or let be.
Bent & folded downward lies say a path of
infinite truth.
As a sequence, series of pattern & disarray,
infinitesimal dust closes the extent of space and time.
The infectious ash of ghosts or
minute wonders of diminished capacity
as a sparrow swift in gale—of monsoon wind.
A sparring sparrow whipping, and whirring downward
to most not dying with wings,
flipping, slapping the water
as it rises to mitosis or meiosis,
luster in the division of methane.
A man or a woman duplicated or divided into two.
A man or a woman duplicated in nothingness
of pure carbon, oxygen, nitrogen, with a lumen life.

Song of Blood Mosquito Dance

On air thick morning fog as her wing song whirred,
bringing him around closer. She smelled of blood
roses as her black-striped stomach bloated & red, red.

Mosquito man liked her natural faceted eyes close.
Her needle nose like a straw for blood & tool for life.
He likes her sway to the music made with her wings.

Her cousins would sing her asleep by their
own cicada rhythms & throat songs, a gentle hum deep.
However, Inupiaq forgot and feared such singsongs.

Wet, heavy air dousing down rain   warm & wavering
A sunbow in the distant   space of crystal sonata
shine. This is where sparrows and hummingbirds come.

A time of breeding is on all the minds of mosquitoes.
It is in perfect synchronicity of wings, the coming together,
each whir a note of motion: & in a moment Gone. Gone.

Fasting 7 moons and suns out Cache Creek way on
a mountain, in Shuswap country, at Sugar Kane abysmal
in Yukon territory. In forest realms we kneel listened and heard.

Swarms of mosquito came to me but did not leave, instead they swarmed. I listened intently to what was told in song.

I dreamed of me & you:

> Listen by hearing with your inua,
> for I want you to hear with no ego.
> I need you to know what you need
> and need what you know. Sing to others
> in sacredness & grace. You may call on
> me to be your helper mosquito, in Utqiagvik.
> Maybe you will help others deal or cope
> with historical grief or loss. Sister believe
> me & pay attention for yourself, sing this song
> always, it is yours now. When needed for
> yourself to heal & heal many, sing hard.

I sang her song with her only once with gut and heart. We opened our eyes, & were in flight all around us mosquitoes but, only the female. My stomach red, and striped, my wings iridescently whirring. We sing louder and feel good & clean. Her new song in my throat it vibrates, for she is feeding her eggs while drinking blood, giving life a chance.

When the Mosquitoes Came

As mosquitoes came north, the swarm dark and clouded,
pollack bones left on the river's shore discarded by thrill
of the line or by love left late,
softened and hardened the babies already in their genes
didn't appear all in one sitting, no.
Adoption was forced, fought over with words exchanged,
mostly big, large words.
Inupiat links sentences.
No, not all at once did they come,
those takers didn't know. Then they came in waves of time,
curiosity driven in urgency of a newborn baby girl,
me to be only theirs, no matter what harm it caused me
it was to an Inupiaq family secret,
what they knew meant right makes might.
New parents: baby blankets, cotton diapers,
baby wash, baby oil and baby creator.
Somewhere on the old dirt road I understood who they were.
Mom and Dad. Government hardworking adoptive parents
or, as their nicknames, the mosquito people.
Military action, do-gooders, the church, the takers of blood-kin.
In imagination and pure, and blood of gut.
Intuition from genetic memory, I don't know.
Something happened the day of the welts,

my cord attached to my mother is cut.

Once fasting on Mount Williwaw I was bitten 340 times.

The mosquito bites became welts, festering and bloody.

In an agitated trance of insect song,

mischievously I squeezed my flesh on either side.

While they were biting, they exploded.

I did it again. Repeatedly. Explosion! Explosion! I watched them pop.

I felt insane and cruel of my blood and the mosquito squeamishly excited.

The mosquitoes gorged and I felt odd, so I quit.

They still foraged my body, left pockmarks to nourish their eggs.

Blood is for the female to aid, for she siphons blood,

not the male mosquito. He goes elsewhere to feed.

Of pollen flowers, young blood.

Found

Taken:

duck foot skin;
an owl with five owlets;
nesting minks;
caught in a fish trap.
A bird egg found in winter.

Given:

an Inupiat dictionary left on a rock
by Simon Taargrack Jr.

Eyes in masks left to wear. On my head.
See what is found.

I Want to Believe

I believe when the body is at ruin,
the mind seems to give in to the notion,
blossoms growing out of the ailing part;
at times it's spiritual upheaval, like shoveling
from parts unknown:

> cavities of petunias,
> pistils of bear grass,
> stamens of indian paints,
> ovules of Mozart's string quartets,

but at the moment of morphine
spiraling you can become clear
of one thing.

The wonder of things:

> A mean planet,
> horses running
> hock & fetlock fitly,
> across dirt trails.

In an interval of a minute, momentarily
contained notes on a two-line bar is enough.
Enough pain. Enough crying. Enough settling in.
Enough headaches & certainly enough illness.

Camouflage

FOR JEN

A poising
swallowtail:
with loppy
wings lands;
to honey sip
nectar
on my day
lilies.
Yellow
trumpet
petals;
spotted;
merges
silent and bright;
yellow on yellow
alights;
any red rose
to orange pink.

Thrush's Melody

The unnumbered
sailing stones of Death Valley
thrush's melody beat her/my skin with increased throb.
Thrice bitten by a sand flea storm,
could never stop the throes
of convulsions as today's exoplanet.
She/I unwoven as we enter the north
and south pole transpiring-in-zone.
Our mind became flight!
She/I of double women shades,
with the song thrush's melody,
wearing a double shroud
over the land of dead-eyed people
of no sound, a dimension of lyric pushing
the ridge of mental age—say of 428 light-years—
of sentient beings with a refined
conveyance of gesture. STOP. NO!
Not like that, but maybe. We join and conjoin
our inner selves in fire and skull.
No one else can twist the lever of how
it is. A thistle of wild cotton, that ignites
and goes rogue is a volcano with lava
map charts unfold the tectonic plates,
yield to sea light, sing thrush sing
for snow and twenty-five below.

Drum

FOR FEATHER

As sparrow bore sand down
songs clamored.   Abstruse:
black-leaf Russian tobacco;
felt through her/my fingers.
The sill of the window chipping,
opacity-shade, with rice-paper
blinds, newspapers with no dates.
Convulsing on the concrete,
our opaque, thick heart, expels—
the darting demon sick; embodied
in my baptized breasts—
exorcise me, where 4 valves
blood-a-beat.

Physical Thaw

I taste
Berries and roots
Polar cap   ice melt,
Swamp algae,
moose tracks,
covered dripping,
chartreuse moss,
rocks,
it reminds me of,
my collapsed veins,
IV   drip drip drip,
right arm,
restricted appendage,
pink-tan-blue
like frozen to liquid
freed from bodily
frost   thaw under sunbaked
paper birch peelings
I peel back the blood loss
of sunbaked leaves above.
Roaring sun
wax   wick   wax wick
calves my   tachycardia   fastest.

No more   liquid to quench.
I double   leg   cramp.
My throat craves more   melt water
as I candle the seal-oil lamp
again again
again.

Fuse

In I follow the Little People,
descending on stone steps:
a labyrinth ready to unfold
its thorns, blossoms, rugged roots.
I dwell in the mind of damper ground,
an investigation, a spell, in the 6,228 ft.
hole of methane. Listen to the thaw in the spongy
depths of a quantum multiverse; of silver
globules rising, in the air-lunged
permafrost—floating—floating above,
Little People on the backs of bowheads,
carrying a rusted steel box of olden tools.
Shasta daisies lend beauty to sedges
and moss cradles the Quonset hut.

                    razor cut flayed flesh
                    lies on the cold cement floor
                    of symbols fuse me

Dear Mommie, (I'm sick)

She/I in a drab goose-wing suit create recall backlash throwing
ice-wintered rocks to the outhouse mirror.
The track lights, one broken and dangling, above glass reflecting,
a stainless calf and cow moose in shifting shards crackle. Our features
one eye drooping in dizziness, I weigh 85 lb., now. She/I fall in littered snow out the
nailed door half-broken splitting like a dory boat. We span our face She/I.
After years of sun on a Shishmaref Island, snow and glass blended with a stroke of a
brush, red blood acrylic as Picasso's blues, our skin, hair, eyebrows frosted in seconds:
frozen. It's framed as a taffeta float of air in the rosebud blood snow we see a split lip,
cut cheek, ripped nostril at ground zero. On the top of the Arctic Circle no one cares
or in Anchorage nobody shares these jet-powered fly suits, the brown fading to tan
which carry us through the night down dusk. 1,000 miles of adrenaline a suicidal twist
of the head might end, the raped tongue, gums so ready to tell. But the shame might
also die. She/I we look from the dead ground up at the pole-lights. This activity of
clinging to life like putting on a parachute. She/I get up again on lithium. What an
8 × 10 picture never taken so typical in this isolation of bleeding and bruising at mile-
post 165.

Skinny Boned Bear

No fear, dead on in the night sky
Or stuck on the deep web, bear
stars still exist. Name the bone pile.
On the marsh heaving like the
Chukchi Sea: pure white ice & arctic,
Arctic air. 50 miles of open water,
floating, I see a half carcass, marrow bones.
At 5× a black bear, 1,500 lb., 9 feet
tall & with one swipe of his paw—
I'm neck-snapped to the slush ice.
Cheek Blood Snow. I glance across
the whiteness a radio-collared skinny
boned, muddy male polar bear.

        Bones on inner ice
        Melt water tears reflected
        No ice, no seal sharks.

Ernest's Red Knots at Ikpikpuk River

Ernest ties a red string so it's knotted into a ladder.
Clove hitch and bowline to design figures he practices.

Whatever happens Ernest ready for the untangling.

Groomed by his own thoughts his healing stories come.
An old man showed him the ways of flights to the sky.

And how to bring back ash from *embers*,
which fight the water-colored toxins of disease and ailments.

A yellow-billed woodpecker throttles out a deep song from a muskeg.
Flocks grow fragrant. Ernest hears miles away

the solar shift and his left eye twitches.
He knows this swaying and the change or exchange.

He walks down to Ship Creek, a brook lives
in his mind for years as a puny trickle from the drying air.

Whenever Ernest goes raptor hunting he goes to the creek
and collects eggs, to groom the hatchlings, to bring back water.

Like at *Ikpikpuk* river caterwauling a pair of tundra swans,
he's drawn to feathers to wear on his mask: always healing.

Ernest cops a landing graceful he's yet sore and stiff,
from the long bleak flight, taken so far away in slumber.

Ernest's fist flings the dart, it wraps and wraps a noose
on the gray, rough-necked, Steller's vultures, it goes limp.

Ernest's bird dart tied with red knots secure and taut,
keep him healing with many full goosefeet baskets.

Her New Moon Enigma

FOR ANNE WALDMAN

The Katmai Mountains encircle an arctic valley of ash,
she/I call/s a *dark female enigma* to arise slow.

She engulfs us with her volcanic scorch effortlessly,
as a redshifting web tangles the universe.

Her fireweed gossamer fills the taiga fields,
as myriad, silt waves slither like white, snow snakes.

One meditation: *OOMMM* sings a thousand vibrations
puffing ten-thousand smoke rings as time is upside down.

The sand is a sluice gate bolted shut.
A deadlocked spindle in a ratchet spins, spins.

She/I can call on her earnestly for tenacity of all
Gossamurmur knowing longevity of ageless buds.

Gauze rings of energy as catabolics
consider: a cocooned lady/I

and *the great female enigma*: allows the entrance
into her/me as a threshold of the infinite time,

which blooms of exoplanet roses with thorn stars.
We all enter three in the one of anabolic measures

of activity which culminates in ice as the nurturing
of creation melting as her/my out-of-mind time.

Out of cold minutes dressed in a goose-feathered
Inupiaq parka as we feel all the oceans rising

sloshing and quaking,
the firmament heaving,

the arctic cotton flying,
pupas unraveling,

gypsy moths' nests falling,
then   regenerating and sparkling

tissues of   blood bone brains
cells   tendons   tightening
her might is the silken sinew of caribou back-straps
which carry her/I with the dark female enigma
into the stratopause zone of deep dropping

in altitude and temperatures of 31 to 34 miles
where all things change into a serene new moon

Atigiluk Armor

I breast-scan the deciduous yellow aspen
the trees of monsoon hail.
Then with the rains come—water
evaporating fast—lightning
bolt spikes. I see a woman in her atigiluk
dress—wet and freezing rusted ice
chains of Chemotherapy IV tubing.
I knew her in calico armor from Barrow,
but she wasn't in my igloo of arctic ice,
she's in a desert the Hogan Cancer
Institute, and she's so thirsty for water.
Oh! The garden gates of life and death!
The seven o'clock flowered earth,
which has its time to bloom in succulent
pink. In homes of clay straw or sod houses
diminish to effigy dust as ashes turn to ash.
She falls into water in a ritual of dance,
conjuring round prayer—wishing for life.
I two-step in maklaks while stroking
the walrus intestine drum—not for myself,
but for those who cannot dance
and those of no breasts.
Slippery rocky riverbeds share with us
ninety-eight percent water.

I carve sitting on granite
rocks with Inuit goggles on,
for looking through the light
lenses to see
our stark and naked
hollow-breasted bodies.
In my inua spirit;
this essence rises
like the old ones.

Warm Water Fish Moving In

Out there, believing a spiritual ruin
the body passes & the dead found scavenged
hock to fetlock, on these beaches.
The body rests on round patches
of dried sea grasses.
Out there, the night entrance looms
from earthly, inward, silent escapes
like sound shapes
of the cosmos swirling.
The wall of salt-white chance.
I tap lightly like an alderfly.

Upon cool, damp ground
I throw stones half-halt. TSTHHsssHHH!
Pebbles quickly fly windward
restraining the nightglow livery.
A freehold. I hang on the seaside banister.
For here: my ears bleed like a cat's
in the evening; my nose hears instinct; my eyes smell salt!
I crouch to the ocean's ocean watching waves fold & spray.
Fold & spray

Here: in bone-shackled shells;
around my flowered bound hands;

tightly held—still my free feet walk

as a beetle across a sidewalk.

I find: the dead spot of the fawn lily;

three human heads; dusty; tampered; stilted;

like dried up blossoms. But, black on blue.

Out there: dust particles; a somber,

solar moon waning; & beetle browed.

Large dome ice cores wake the dead

living to the time & hour of melting

igloos & ice caves, rising butter clams clamped

shut rotten & rancid. Out there, I find albino black grouse huddled in covens.

Here bull thistle in my intestines,

toxic shock & fodder in my seal poke side bag.

Slung over my shoulder

a grimace of a mask peeking at me.

And here, harbor seal walks upright,

porpoise circle the screech wail hides, at the back of my mouth, in here.

Unblinking pupils of owls live. There moon trips grow dark—

here the annual growth of a fish scale is 33 inches.

Fine debris of rocks scatters

bluest eggs of magpies, cobalt.

Enclosed by a caribou herd

in protection like a nest

weaved to the spruce.

And here we polish lying in snow

our bodies to purify or free

of fleas and louse.

In here, I peel off a bony cast

on my head & the temporary loss

of my soul person lives freely.

Here I am not woman or man,

the corpse is played out before life.

I find finger fish holes.

Here like cancer a jar of oil is 21 dollars

a liter & might be 10,400,320 years old.

I intoned her, I purse my lips

I am pursued by my eye shape.

Herehereherehereherehere again

my coverlid & domed mind

hides under closed eyes

feels the warm water of fish

moving moving in.

When White Hawks Come

I dreamt the spirit of the codfish:

in rafters of the mind;

fly out into the winter's blue night;

mirth off alder tendrils sashay;

while I set up my winter tent;

four panels long—beams suspend

blubber strips aged in a poke seal bag;

a bluejay lands on the windowsill wing feathers—

shadowing the sun as a new moon; as blue, lapis

icicle time melts—when white hawks come.

She/I Tumble with Old Squaw Duck

Time as a Japanese Coke bottle float

$\qquad\qquad\qquad$ bobbing the ocean surface

Anywhere $\qquad$ but on the shore of Kivalina.

$\qquad$ A number as time is labeled

It reads: *parallelism is not a question but a space* $\quad$ *here*

I am a   woman of time $\qquad\qquad$ a wormhole vacuum

I travel every 4 days $\qquad$ on a walkabout

Between two events $\qquad$ one 10,923 days ago

$\qquad$ one: here & now

$\qquad\qquad\qquad$ now   using the speed of light

$\qquad$ a glow spark casting off in the solar dust

I like to wander $\qquad$ to find things

$\qquad\qquad\qquad\qquad$ a pretty rock

$\qquad\qquad\qquad\qquad$ a shell

$\qquad\qquad\qquad\qquad$ a slice of baleen

On this shoreline $\qquad$ in this time $\quad$ here in a karigi

$\qquad$ At a ceremonial dance for snow,

I carry a clock watch, round my head in a locket.
I carry light. My feet shine step into this place.

I see an acrobatic lady of the plants she gives me medicine
In her DNA she preprogrammed with 2,117 nanoseconds of seed knowledge

Her carved microcrystalline murmurs through   this taiga
She is named Old Squaw Duck   tossed and tumbled
        at a   blanket toss
                                            in Kivalina.

Grave Posts

Grave Posts:

a painted drum;

carved spirit;

over seal heads of wooden,

caribou galloping;

a man rowing a kayak;

red painted stilts;

on a barren hillside;

bring me to life-shine;

depillared—

as decay grows from human

to one ginkgo tree;

in tall grass;

where raven caws.

Oil Energy & Natural Gas

She fishing   in the mountains   of the Brooks Range

She/I churn: hallowed antlers of many moose   mountain goat;

Dall sheep gruff   claps of beaver tails   stir   Teshekpuk lake.

Caged sand flats   a carcass   thick pussy willow in a drought-

dried lake   no bush willows.

In a bloated   sidewalk say in   Houston, Texas   (Don't Drink the Water)

the water tastes   so fresh   cut with chlorine & natural gas

wake up, Houston   She/I listen to rush hour horns

in an acrid crude daze   with weight of smog   we'll break through the ice

it will freeze and thaw   and another 112 caribou risking

              something new cross the lake break through;

swim and get to the other side   of the shore looking for moss;

20 feet more   legs cramping   we lie down   to rest and die

Blood Snow at Cambridge Bay

She/I   trekked 150 miles   to find   caribou

a young hunter   coming   into an earth mound   cabin

          Hoarfrost

a seal-skinned umiaq   our ABC crew   beached at 70 below 0

An Inua as in an egg   resident spirit being

          fire inside   sweltering thoughts

dis   connect   edly

in   and   out

of

auroras   magnetic   red dust   searing

a blessing

to the Beaufort Sea

a blessing burning   don't melt

melting   don't tell

I see an ice-star

trans- trans- cendent

She/I   change masks into a   musk oxen   don't tell

pull the hemp rope

sliding

down

down

leaving behind   Polaris's   crystal flakes

She/I   die   leaving behind   Polaris's   crystal flakes

at   Cambridge Bay   cabin

ACKNOWLEDGMENTS

Taku ila. Thank you to the great spirit. I'd like to thank the following people and organizations: Arthur Sze, Jackie and Richard Neel, Jennifer Foerster, Sherwin Bitsui, Layli Long Soldier, Britta Anderson, Heather Cahoon, Jode and Juan Perez, Linda Ferris, Corwin Claremont, Roy Big Crane, Joy Harjo, Brandy Lee Miller, Nellie O'Neil, the Cahoon family, Liv Perez, Denise de la Cruz, Cedar Sigo, Linda Hummingbird, and Tracy K. Smith. Especially, Joshua Beckman.

I'd also like to thank the following organizations: *Poetry* magazine, the Academy of American Poets, the Institute of American Indian Arts, the American Academy of Arts and Sciences, Salish Kootenai College, Cook Inlet Region Inc., and Wave Books.